34th Street
and other poems
(1982-1984)

Books by Carlota Caulfield

Fanaim
Sometimes I Call Myself Childhood
Oscuridad Divina
El tiempo es una mujer que espera

Carlota Caulfield

34th Street
and other poems
(1982-1984)

Translated by Chris Allen and the author

Preface by Jack Foley

Eboli Poetry Series
San Francisco

Some of the poems in this book have appeared in *Palabra Solar*, *Termino Magazine*, and *Poetry San Francisco*. The poems " A job in New York," "My Grandfather's Currach," "You All Know The Story of the Two Lovers," "GG," "Love with You is Tiresome Work," and "The Ballad of Laszlo" were written in English by the author.

Photo of the author by Servando Gonzalez
Typesetting by *Ediciones El Gato Tuerto*
San Francisco, California.

Library of Congress Catalog Card Number 87-80166
ISBN 0-932-36708-9

EDICIONES EL GATO TUERTO
P.O. Box 210277
San Francisco, Ca. 94121
USA

For my mother

CONTENTS

PREFACE

The opening poem of Garcia Lorca's *Poeta en Nueva York* begins, "Asesinado por el cielo," murdered by the sky, by heaven. The powerful surrealistic impulse of Lorca's poetry represents at once a response to and an escape from the horrors of the modern city. In contrast, Carlota Caulfield's **34th Street** begins by zeroing in on what is almost tenderly referred to as "a little spot on the map":

> Thirty-Fourth Street in the Greek quarter
> Of New York opens its gates.

The poem is full of sharply-observed physical details -the rocking chairs, the "ubiquitous radios," the "laundry-lines"- details which at times "take off" in a surrealism which is as telling as but far gentler than Lorca's: "The rocking chairs jump into an infinity / Of concrete." Yet it is perhaps the *sounds* of 34th Street which most engage the poet's attention: "ubiquitous radios blare away untiringly," "football games turned up full-blast." The neighborhood is, as she describes it, "Boxed in, I5 minutes from Babel," the *Greek* quarter though there are other "quarters," other languages to be heard as well. Like Lorca, the poet is almost physically assaulted by the city -"Hundreds of children erupt daily"- yet, unlike Lorca, Caulfield admits that the city is, after all, "where I live," the place, as she puts it in "The Babel of Iron," "where our lives are." Lorca's book ends in a tremendous yearning for the very place Carlota Caulfield comes from -for Cuba:

> *Cuando llegue la luna llena iré a Santiago de Cuba,*
> *iré a Santiago,*
> *en un coche de agua negra.*
> *Iré a Santiago.*

> When the full moon arrives, I'll go to Santiago de Cuba,
> I'll go to Santiago
> in a coach of black water.
> I'll go to Santiago.

But for this poet no such escape to an idealized "place" is possible. The opening of her book marks the beginning of what she will call in a moment her "tremendous solitude of exile."

And yet: perhaps not so solitary after all:

> What has New York been for me?
> A city seen in your eyes.*

Though Carlota Caulfield realizes very well the imaginary quality of places like Lorca's "Cuba" (see "My Grandfather's Currach" or the comments on "That quasi-divine universal paradise" in "The Babel of Iron") there is nevertheless in her work "a *place* set aside / in remembrance" (my italics). The concluding poem of the New York section of the book is addressed to an American writer with a Portuguese surname, a writer whose family history encompassed the problem of the immigrant. In it she asserts not only that she is "beginning to love New York" -one can hardly imagine Lorca asserting that!- but that "The poet lives on dreams written / in books." Like Lewis Carroll's Alice, Carlota Caulfield seems to have immediate access to another world, a world which she can enter either "through the keyhole of memories" (she speaks in one poem of "my wild memory") or through "dream." "I dream you," she writes, "I feel you." In Carlota Caulfield's work the poet is in exile not only from Cuba but from childhood, from all beginnings. "How does one get to the center / of things?" she asks. She asserts herself to be Jewish ("Catholic-jew myself"), Irish, Cuban; her father spoke German. She speaks of herself as condemned to the status of the wanderer -"condemned to bear the sign of Cain"- and writes a poem to Abraxas, according to some traditions the most ancient of gods, the source of the word, "Abracadabra," according to others a particularly potent demon often pictured carrying a whip! It is this fundamental exile -the exile of the imaginative person at large in the world- which is the source of all her other exiles:

> When I was a child
> I liked to play with the sky,
> To walk looking upwards,
> To spin around until I fell down...

And yet: "I haven't stopped being a child." These poems revolve with great richness around themes of memory, exile, love, childhood, dreams. In her beautiful poem about Orpheus and Eurydice the two lovers remain delicately poised, endlessly separated, yet, through the power of deep imagination, endlessly connected:

> Today Eurydice played
> With the labyrinthine earth
> And imagined herself
> Bound to Orpheus' skin
> Imagined herself...
> Somewhere inside him.

> Today Orpheus played
> With his hands
> And imagined himself
> Playing a drum
> Somewhere inside
> Eurydice's intermittent city.

It is Carlota Caulfield's extraordinary ability to remain in that precise state -at once separated and connected, exiled and "at home"- that gives her work its special poignancy and joy, its special power. All of these elements come into play in her marvelous poem about her "Grandfather's Currach." Everything about the Irish grandfather (born in Gibraltar) manifests his Irish roots. One day he has a "revelation" about a special place, "a figment of Eire's imagination," and off he goes into the sea, becoming the wanderer. The poet assures her grandfather that she has her own "currach" (Gaelic, canoe), and that at the moment of her death -the moment of exile from everything- she, her father, and her grandfather will be reunited:

I have my canoe, Grandfather,
And when I die,
The three of us-
And only we three-
Will go dance a Ceili
In the middle of the sea.

   This book is Carlota Caulfield's invitation to the reader to "dance a Ceili" with her. It is a deep pleasure to accept the invitation.

3/2/87

Jack Foley

---

* In Lorca eroticism manifests itself through huge mythic figures such as "the king of Harlem" or "Walt Whitman," figures of enormous energy capable of breaking through the anguish and oppression Lorca finds all around him. ("New York of slime, / New York of wires and of death.") In Caulfield eroticism involves a very real lover with very real problems ("You are returning to your wife and...").

I
THE MOVIOLA HAS A CRUDE SOUND SYSTEM

Houses in a row, houses in a row,
Houses in a row.

Alfonsina   Storni

34TH STREET (A LITTLE SPOT ON THE MAP)

Thirty-Fourth Street in the Greek quarter

Of New York opens its gates.

The rocking chairs jump into an infinity

Of concrete.

From afternoon winter silence,

Hundreds of children erupt daily.

The ubiquitious radios blare away untiringly.

Hidden laundry-lines are

Like arms for the walls.

The army of bricks repeats itself

As far as the horizon

As the living image of the first settlers here.

Thirty-Fourth Street in Astoria

In a banal neighborhood,

A narrow passageway giving shelter to the poor,

To cheapskates, to anyone hanging out.

Broadway nearby with aromas of figs,

Of souvlaki, of taverns,

Of football games turned up full-blast

In the Deli around the corner.

Thirty-Fourth Street. The smell of feta.

A shot of brandy yesterday with the Galicians,

The calls of Jose and Stavros

In the early summer air.

Thirty-Fourth Street in the Greek quarter,

Boxed in, 15 minutes from Babel.

And let's add: 31-52, where I live.

THE BABEL OF IRON

Through a dirty, old, broken window,
I look at the red brick buildings,
The image of a lost city, which
-as has already happened-
Can still save itself.

Your dreams always dwelt on
Those stories of your friend Hurtado,
Years of miracle-working,
Of filling your stomach with ten cents,
Of having lots of luck and hope.

That quasi-divine universal paradise
Nourished the blood of whole peoples,
Laved the heads of the bold every day,
Was the faithful friend at breakfast,
Became their lover in bed at night.

To work on Fifth Avenue was to be in heaven:
Selling ties, buying a hotel,
To be rolling in money.
Facile things.

But the times have changed.

They're so different, so odd;

At the same time, the same.

People are the same; the waiting, the same.

Luck is the same, and the book of fate,

The same.

The suffering of the immigrants hasn't changed.

Irish, Greeks, Italians,

Jews, Cubans, Salvadorians...

All taken for dogs at one time or another.

History repeats itself.

People are the same everywhere.

Through a dirty, old, broken window,

I see the skyscrapers of an illusion

And the path traced since the beginning,

Where our lives are.

THE SPRING IS OVER

and my heart began to open then,
trying to find the beginning of my life.
i was tired.
my hands.
my soul.

a bird with its surprising beak
startled the glass without giving me warning.
the air resounded
and copper sang timidly
in the labyrinths of dreams.

my body voyaged everywhere
but i had a place set aside
in remembrance.

the early-morning hour touched my face
and nothingness spilled
onto the ceiling of my room.

behind preoccupations

i began to pulsate

even in the futon where i sleep.

i was thanked by the grimy cat in the window

and this tremendous solitude of exile

and a few poems, paper enclosed

like a staircase,

made up my intrinsic immortality.

ABRAXAS AND I

You're always around
Like the music of an organ.
Wind without ethics
Hair without morals.
Wrapping yourself around my legs.
Here you are
With your eyes fixed on my skin
I, condemned to bear the sign of Cain
You, condemned not to die.

I begin to be the winged thing
Because you lean over my back
Sinking your teeth into me.
I, with sleeping passions,
You, fecund and beautiful.

To the tune of the organ
"The great bird destroys the rattlesnake."
Your hands move
"The world is an egg."
And from your throat bursts a cry
"The bird flies toward God."

Here is my name Abraxas.

A FRIDAY

What can we say about Time?

What can we say about being Time?

Autumn hums its first chills

The lark dreams about listening to children

Silence is as gigantic

As a Sunday in my heart.

And squirrels leap under the leaves

Fall and fly, halt, and begin the game again.

Where are you, my love?

Where can I feel your hands?

It's already late,

And I don't want to be a friend of Time.

LOVE

I

A portion of air came with its clothes open
Out came the arbor's smile-   a smile
of distilled spirits.
A dog appeared. The cat smiled. I saw you.

II

On top of a tree in Westchester,
a blackbird sings.
But I have no house, not even my own window
to see it.
And cheer myself up. Nor desires.

The river opens its bed.
The grass tickles my skin.
Unseeing, I walk.

I dream you, I feel you,
and when I have my own empty space,
I will fly a Japanese kite.

A POEM

I.

Out of the dark silence of the god Mars
Penetrated to the inner depths
by the invisible seed
Marked by a Buddha's navel
shattered into splinters;
After listening to all,
Vulgar words in my ears
Misused names for each thing,
Your shadow behind them
Your brief name vibrating in the shadow.

II.

Nothing matters. Nothing matters any more.

III.

Life is a fragment full of the unexpected
Sometimes so ill-finished that it frightens.
It won't stop biting; biting hard,
Until it chews a ravine in your soul.

IV.

If I raise my feet, my ambitions tickle me.
It becomes so enjoyable to imagine...
and imagine again.
And you watch me. I, I think, I think.

CRONICON

And when the elephants lost the tracks,
And nothing could be done,
While their trunks ran around the treadmill,
A speck fell from the air
And the elephants rediscovered their traces.

WHAT CAN WE DO THEN?

And if your eyes look afar
If we can't send elephants
If we can't escape from the scribbles
Of the days
What can we do then?

A JOB IN NEW YORK

To Gertrude Stein

the morning sparrows gone,

the sound of GG to Br'klyn.

my soul with the autumn constellations

IT'S A JOB!

i need to blow it all to hell and gone

THAT'S THE JOB!

a video tape recorder in Forest Hills

one unicorn trying to enjoy life

and my heart young and happy.

a squirrel in the green

the old church under the tea tree.

the evening arrives:

we look up and it is there

the rain in my window,

WHAT A JOB!

and the last hour of my time

had voices in the dream

36TH STREET

IS A JOB, IS A JOB, IS A JOB, IS

GG

GG to Br'klyn
Today is like yesterday
No present no future
Heute is gestern

GG to Asdor
El as de las gafas
L'as des lunettes
Das As der Brillen
The Ace- The Best of Glasses
GG to Br'klyn
Tea and coffee free
(only downstairs)
thirty minutes lunch
no take more, no more, no more
bring up the elevator!
pick up the intercom!

You, my life in your hands
You, again in free days

Place of Jewish heroes

Catholic-Jew myself

With a nice violin

With Hungarian words

You too, Abe

And the day will be over in a minute

GG to bread

GG to immortality

Kaufen Sie frames!

Asdor, the king

DAS ACE DE LAS LUNETTES...............

YOU ALL KNOW THE STORY
OF THE TWO LOVERS

Today Eurydice played
With the labyrinthine earth
And imagined herself
Bound to Orpheus' skin
Imagined herself...
Somewhere inside him.

Today Orpheus played
With his hands
And imagined himself
Playing a drum
Somewhere inside
Eurydice's intermittent city.

LOVE WITH YOU IS TIRESOME WORK

My eyes reflect your tenderness
In each corner of the fleeting day,
While you are lost in others
And I make you real
Until the moment you look at me
From the "immense distance"
Between my chair and table
And the five feet away, where you're
Making a cup of coffee.

How many times have I used my wild memory
In these days of so much love
And toyed with the idea of your pleasure

And here you are coming into harbor
(Love with you
Is like jumping on and off
A merry-go-round)

The sound of your body
Is a needle that stitches my skin
With more desire.

(You are returning to your wife and
I have never wanted to break
The supposed perfection
Of your live
I ask nothing of you
Your many fears divert me)

You would read this letter
In your best voice
(I try to hide my desire
To possess you)

I only want us to be
A man and a woman
At one
With the prancing horses.

What has New York been for me?
A city seen in your eyes

TO JOHN DOS PASSOS

Following the path of Manhattan Transfer

The odor of onions seeps from the heart
of this city,
The poet lives on dreams written
in books,
And the old cemetery makes a shadow
At the end
of the street.

Nothing has been lost. This time
there are few pigeons,
But the sound of the steamship can be felt
with your feet,
The air burns in your ears
Scarfs fly off and take the place
of handkerchiefs.

Frankfurters make us hungry
Click, clak, clik, clak,
the chesnuts play.

The man with the accordeon creates images,
And people dance, sing and live.

It's Sunday
The Staten Island Ferry is full.
I'm beginning to love New York.

I trace the path on the map.
"How does one get to the center
of things?"

The shells stay in the sea.
The black hat flies over Battery Park
Feet push forward through garbage.
The wind pushes. The quiet corners
Of Wall Street
capriciously blend together.
Someone asks something in German-American.

The years of the twenties
Emerge in the memory of my father.

II
THROUGH THE KEYHOLE OF MEMORIES

FOR MY FATHER

You who lived walking over time
Majestic of skin and of soul. You
Whom solitude made into a god,
I remember your ancestral darknesses,
Dreaming dreams of what you never hoped for,
The roads without final prayers,
The accursed tranquillity which cut our wings,
I saw you die. It was that morning
When I began to be nobody.

MY GRANDFATHER'S CURRACH

The day you had the revelation of Hy-Brasail,
That lost land of eternal youth and happiness,
Peace ended in your soul.

Grandfather, how did it occur to you
To be born in Gibraltar?

The day your father gave you
Your first pampooties
Made with the crude leather of the Irish soil,
You seemed to see them sleeping forever
In the trunk.

Tell me, Grandfather, why did you go to Paris?

With the dreamer's refusal to conform
Your *Ubi bene, ibi patria* disintegrated
With that piratical smile
Playing in the warehouse of military hardware.

And who would tell you, dear Grandfather,

That from the Rock you would sally

Without compass or country,

Turned into a Count's secretary,

Under the spell of the smell of the islands

Captured by your head for generations.

Grandfather, that day that I had my revelation,

When in a dream

I saw your little canoe being built,

You put the pampooties on your feet,

And your tiny bird-of-prey's eyes

Looked at your son and me

To carry us away to that Island

Heaved up every seven years,

A figment of Eire's imagination.

I have my canoe, Grandfather,

And when I die,

The three of us-

And only we three-

Will go dance a Ceili

In the middle of the sea.

BLASA

I looked at myself in your mulatto face
Nanny of my heart
I robbed a piece of rainbow
And bursting with laughter
Locked my seven years
In the blue wooden wardrobe
With the two big mirrors,
A gift from my grandmother;
And I surprised you, almost startled you
When I went out, jumping
Through the keyhole
Until I tickled you... :
That girl of mine!
The combs you wore
Made a noise
In the white foam
Of your hair
While your little eyes
Danced behind
Little tortoises' glasses
And that impeccable dress of yours
Kept the tenderness of our encounter.

Nanny, you and nobody more than you
Gave me poetry.

GIVE ME A KISS AND GO TO SCHOOL

The weeping willow

Consoles itself

With the hummingbird

The playful lizard

Emits color

The aged cat

Tells tales

The gardener

Looks and looks

Let's play hopscotch

So grandmother

Will give us bread and cinnamon

> A la una, mi mula;
> A las dos, mi reloj;
> A las tres, mi café;
> A las cuatro, mi gato
> . . .

ONE OF MY FAVORITE STORIES

Cockroach Martina sings that old song
about dark eyes:
She throws her beauty-mark into the air.
The armchair in the doorway spills out saffron
And her ribbon takes flight with the nap breeze;
Don't give it away to anyone, no, Martina.

Twelve o'clock passes; now it's one,
The sultriness of the day melts
The powder of your face
Nobody's perfect, Cockroach,
You see now
The next to take his turn is Mouse Perez.
The wedding present: a balloon
Honey: in the soup
How pretty you are today!
Want to marry me?
The onion, the tidbit, and the kettle.

Pobrecito el ratón Pérez
que se cayó en la olla
por la golosina
de la cebolla,
y la cucarachita Martina
suspira y llora.

STRUM! STRUM! STRUM!
Goes the guitar.
If you marry an Englishman you're lost,
If your fiancé is Portuguese...

Your beauty-mark sings "Cielito lindo."

Ese lunar
que tienes Cielito Lindo
junto a la boca
No se lo des a nadie
Cielito Lindo
que a mí me toca.

THE BALLAD OF LASZLO

To Sean

If you were Janos Vitez,
Shepherd of snow-fallen sheep,
Turned into clouds,
Carried heavenwards by sorcery,
You would soon forget
The curse love bears with it.
And from your pockets the meadow
Would tumble out like a river,
And the washerwoman's song
Would doom you forever.

Juanito Mazorca, Little John, Janos Vitez,
You well know
What that abrupt love is,
Which, from a dove,
From an unending laugh,
From time unexisting,
Turn into chains
And causes so much hurt.
Janos, you really deserve Petofi's poem.

Voice 1:

You, soldier: twenty-seven episodes
Make up your life.

Oh, Juanito, how beautiful your cape!
What high-heeled boots!

Voice 2:

That dark hair of yours
And that gypsy moustache.
All for love of days gone by,
And with verses, learnt by heart
In your breast.

Janos, you belong to another age.

The death of your beloved broke
The summit of your heart,
And from the ocean, the Giants,
The Dragon, the Fairies,
You yourself became an illusion
Of sanctified Heaven.
In order to change the kiss
Of the Eternal into food for the rainbow
And the Earth,
More than for God's paradise.

Voice 1:

Janos Vitez, more than the harmony
Of your body!

Voice 2:

Your hands, swift as butterflies
With furious passion!

While from one mouth to another
Your name flew to the poet,
Whose heart filled with your images
And who refused to let you die.
Then, hands full of lines and colors,
There was the portraitist
Who made you visible to me.

Voice 1:

If I could write you
Of a thousand sojourns: oh, Janos!

Voice 2:

If they poured like cool water
Out of my heart,

I would sing them all for you.
Now, I can only give these poor,
Fragmentary lines.
Let's see what happens, later.   49

A LITTLE CLOUD PASSES IN THE SKY

They say that clouds are pure secrets
Of children
And that playing hopscotch, hide-and-seek,
"The Queen", and "My house's patio",
Are bygone things.

El patio de mi casa
es particular
que llueve y se moja
como los demás

When I was a child
I liked to play with the sky,
To walk looking upwards,
To spin around until I fell down,
To discover those marvelous clouds
Looking like old men's heads
Curled-up serpents, long noses,
Top hats, sleeping foxes, giant shoes.

And it was so good to play "You see, I see,
I see, ...I see,"
To speak of the snail which leaves for the sun.
And what pleased me most was the song about
Señora Santana which my mother sang
When she sheltered me.

-Señora Santana,
  por qué llora el niño?
-Por una manzana
  que se le ha perdido.

They said that clouds
Are pure secrets of children.
I haven't stopped being a child
So that I won't lose my seven years,
Or "My house's patio."

When I walked hand-in-hand with my father
Through the streets of Old Havana,
The little Chinese restaurants
Showed their red-and-white checked tablecloths
And the oyster-stands looked at each other
From opposite corners.

To go to the *Casa Belga* for books
Was a daily trip.
That passion of mine for pencil-cases,
Colored crayons, and erasers
Crowded into small wooden boxes.

They say that clouds
Are pure secrets of children
And I remember the blue bicycle
With rabbits' tails
And the never-used roller-skates

And the enormous brown piano
And the Pinocchio my aunt
Kept in a narrow wardrobe
And "Ring-Around-The-Rosy"
With bread and cinnamon

> A la Rueda-Rueda
> de pan y canela...

When I was a little girl
I liked bald dolls
I was a friend of two stuffed clowns:
Rasputin and Cachetes.
(I still have the fifties' photo with them)

They say that clouds
              are
                   pure
Secrets of children...